HALLWAY OF MESSAGES

BY
DIANA THORNLEY

AKA

RAINY KNIGHT

IMPRINTS

Published by
Crystal Heart Imprints
Springfield, IL
www.crystalheartimprints.com

All rights reserved
Copyright 2020 by Diana Thornley

Printed in United States of America

Cover Design: Erica Thomas
Interior Design: Ruth Souther

ISBN: 978-1-945567-24-7

HALLWAY OF MESSAGES

DEDICATION & ACKNOWLEDGEMENTS

Thank you to the West Hollywood Children of the Night where innocence and seduction hold hands. Thank you for your runways full of adventure and shattered expectations.

Thank you four legged and nature's willowy charms, virtual landscapes and infinite freeways into surreal reality and manifestation of hope and rage and calm and sane.

Thank you bad love for your torture within twisting words from my heart and soul and expressions of pain.

A special thank you to Writing Rituals of Springfield, IL and especially to Ruth Souther and Crystal Heart Imprints.

Thank you God and to my family for your love and support.

Thank you to all who believed.

Thank you to the Four winds, the Four corners and to the Elements – seas of blue and black sandy beaches. Thank you to the Sky and birds in flight. Thank you Dawn, thank you Light.

We will dream till our curtains are drawn, to the end we will fight. We will see the truth.

Thank you, great Creator for all things bad and good. Inspiration swells in us all. Illuminate our existence, making life worthwhile. A life lived is not a life in vain.

HALLWAY OF MESSAGES

HALLWAY OF MESSAGES

STREET POETRY

HALLWAY OF MESSAGES

Hallway of messages
    Corridor of reasons
Truth prevails
    Darkness speaks
    Strangers listen

    Fountain of truth
Sands of time
    Static glow
    On a mission

        Altered images
Trails of light
    Stones of silence
      Birds in flight

      Cherubs dance
    Angels sing
On a broken branch
    Your memory clings

    Hollowed virtue
  Steamy night
      In mind and soul
You're mine tonight

    Regret and haunting
  Another time
  Hearts in love
      Yours and mine

HALLWAY OF MESSAGES

Tattered in history
memories in vain
separate directions
spilling love like rain

HALLWAY OF MESSAGES

THE BOY

Gimme the boy who sleeps
    with his guitar
I want the one who takes music
    a little too far
Gimme the boy with music in
    his head with a precious lock
a hair and a little underfed

HALLWAY OF MESSAGES

A GIRL

A girl born
   without the curse
of paying her monthly
   dues is blessed with
fertilization and motherhood
has not denied her

HALLWAY OF MESSAGES

SLEEP

You can drain your sleep
    into a little silver cup
Snow White yeah she keeps you up
    Vitamin B and wheat germ
strengthen your starvation diet
    and add to the intensity of
your unplanned riot
    the house of isolation
        caves in around you
    but you have to be alone
        To do what you do

BY DIANA THORNLEY

HALLWAY OF MESSAGES

TEARS

Feeling minute as
an army ant
I succumb to her trenches
inside a webbed fountain
of bleeding tears

HALLWAY OF MESSAGES

THE RIGHT WAY

    I want you to know
    the right way

Have you since renewed your vows
    Separate lust from inevitable passion
Desire instead of aggravated hunger

Maybe it's better the way we are
    let only our minds make love
in the back of a car

Wrapped for hours
    product of an ionic compound
INVITATION TO HEAVEN

    An angel spreads her wings
  making peace offerings
    sink within me till we are free
like a hot airbrush shooting warm colors
    Illustrated perversion align the bathroom stalls
    where secrets pull themselves
out of the woodwork

HALLWAY OF MESSAGES

DISTRACTION

Boll Weevils
Dancing evil
History of the no minds
Together in contact
We mobilize in ideas
A distraction is
the center of attention

HALLWAY OF MESSAGES

STRENGTH

Sun
Warms the flowers
Gives strength to make them grow
Bathing the harvest
Saturating them row by row
Sun warms the Universe
Every living thing
Bringing and taking life
To it we will cling

BY DIANA THORNLEY

HALLWAY OF MESSAGES

DREAMS

Energy always flows in two directions
Highs and lows
So much mental energy
Gushing with vivid sight
But when discoveries aren't put into motion
I'm under a destructive light

I feel so much resentment
A kind of mania
Like a champagne cork ready to blow
Don't know how much longer I'll be in control

The taunting rage inside is
Fighting to be set free
It's fearless tongue and vengeful stalk
Has done its number on me

Let me bust up this room
Break a mirror or two
Twist your fine silver forks to modern art
Yank the closet doors off their track
Shake this chip off my shoulder and off my back

Racing thoughts run through my mind
Speed accelerates with words
Music must bind
Creation and destruction
My head's an idealistic suction

HALLWAY OF MESSAGES

I'll take you with me
Let me show you some things
You've never seen
Journeys in thought
And fanciful dreams

HALLWAY OF MESSAGES

WEBS

Web of fear
Cloak of delight
Enchanting hostess
Of the night
With a soul
Black as tar
Chains of mystery
Laced with light
Make my choosing
Seem just right

HALLWAY OF MESSAGES

UNITY

Cruising down the aisles
    Empty faces crooked smiles
Trusting martyrs in the street
    Stories bleed from
        those you meet
History and lives of
    dope dealer's wives
Separate tongues culturally spoken
        Complexing unity

BY DIANA THORNLEY

HALLWAY OF MESSAGES

SUPPLIER

You have to be able
to trust your supplier
    to bring you
the best of the bad
    You can decode
his arrival on your afternoon flier
    He reroutes the detour
of the mad
    You'll know him,
he'll be dressed in his
    latest monk attire
He's not just
    another passing fad
He'll keep you from
    falling off the narrow wire
with perfect balanced
    combinations you never had

BY DIANA THORNLEY

HALLWAY OF MESSAGES

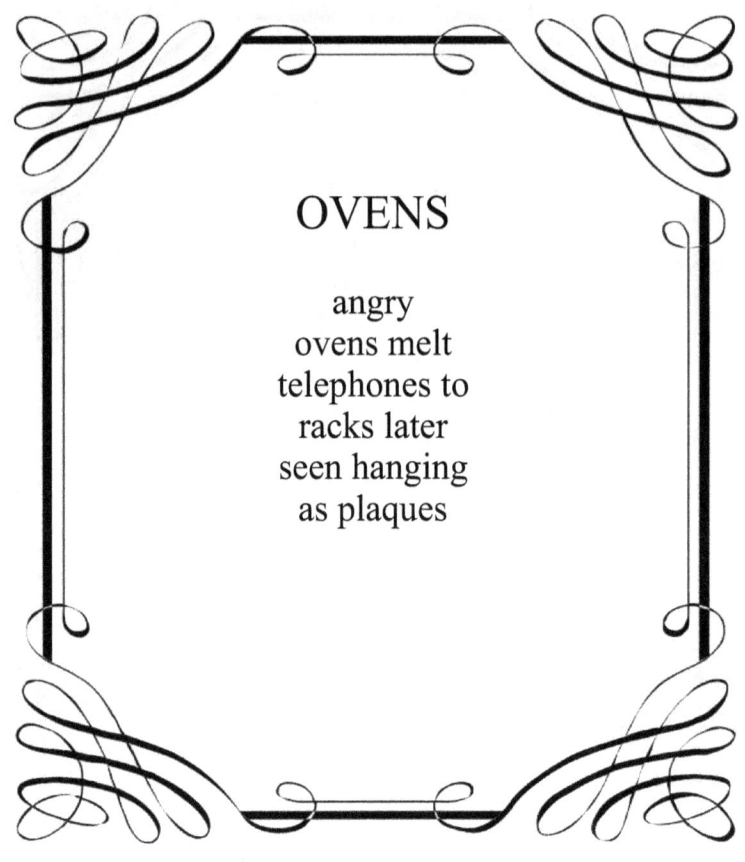

OVENS

angry
ovens melt
telephones to
racks later
seen hanging
as plaques

BY DIANA THORNLEY

PREY

beyond us awaits
the welcoming road
behind lie miles
to loosen that load
gaining in distance
our thoughts go astray
fearing resistance
tears must not display
like a soldier minus array
fighting the challenge:
our prey

HALLWAY OF MESSAGES

OUT

Smoke
Dopeheads
Warheads
Destruction
Burning out

HALLWAY OF MESSAGES

POTATOES

Vegetators
Loafing living
Crippled lives
On couch potatoes

HALLWAY OF MESSAGES

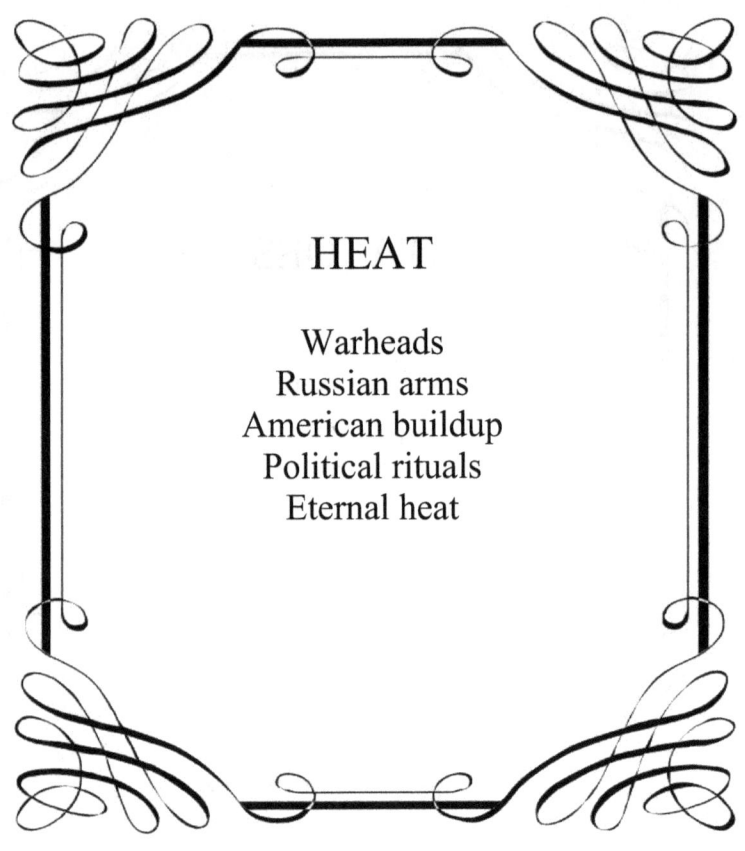

HEAT

Warheads
Russian arms
American buildup
Political rituals
Eternal heat

HALLWAY OF MESSAGES

HUNGER

Famine is the
satiated hunger
of an ascetic's dream

HALLWAY OF MESSAGES

VEINS

Varicose veins
run silently
like muted trains
winding helplessly
seeping crooked lanes
like a webbed fountain
of bleeding tears

HALLWAY OF MESSAGES

SUMMER

yellow maggot
on my beach blanket
hives inject
their stinging bees
inflicting pain
bringing me to my knees

HALLWAY OF MESSAGES

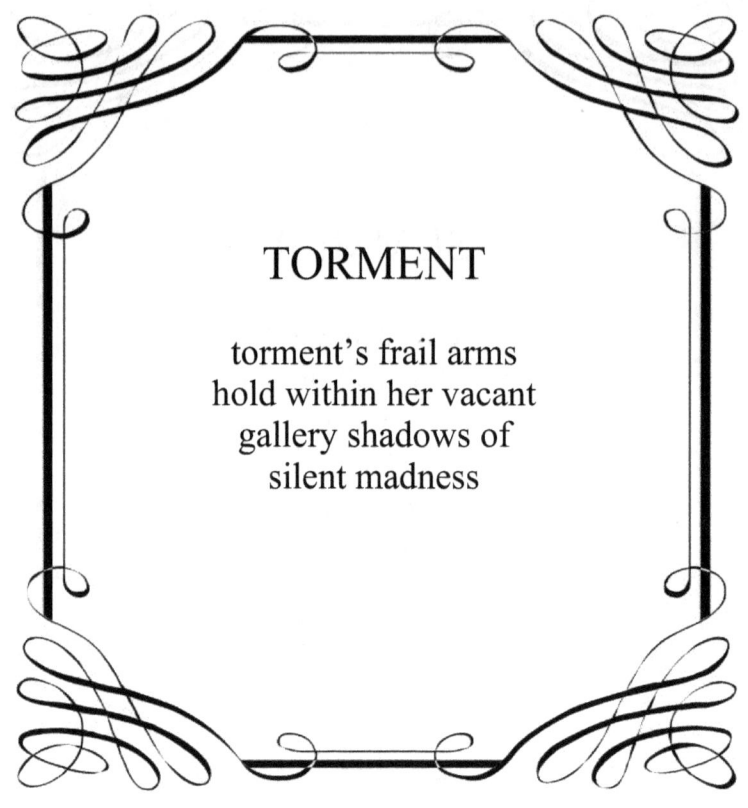

TORMENT

torment's frail arms
hold within her vacant
gallery shadows of
silent madness

HALLWAY OF MESSAGES

SIGNS

no tonal qualities
monotones
no reliances
no matter
give me a sign

HALLWAY OF MESSAGES

YOUR KISS

Your kiss is deep and addictive
as the thirst of the sand
for the rushing waters of the tide
And my hunger for your embrace
is constant and loyal as the sun to the sky

EMOTIONAL EXCHANGE
BEING CONDUCTED
As our sensitivity flourishes
We melt into one another
Uniting into limitless bliss

The power of love is a wonder
Mysticizing as a clash of thunder
Love's chains remain unbroken
By actions and words unspoken

BY DIANA THORNLEY

HALLWAY OF MESSAGES

RAIN

sky shoots rivets
of offbeat rain
like a drummer
playing reggae
on a subway train

HALLWAY OF MESSAGES

SERIOUS LOVE

Serious love
On a serious night
Damsel in demise
Or daughter of light

She-pale in her damask
Singing the minstrel blues
Hoping and praying
He'll say his I do's

Kings and queens and Earthly dreams
Sacred and royal are the genes
Screams of delight
Light versus darkness
Ecstasy against pain
Pouring like a current
No room for disdain

Longing and projecting
And astral highs
The sting and lament of outright lies
Particles of your consciousness
Atoms of its release

Now I understand
Your crush on my niece
Radical departure
Head loom of peace
Don't aske me to
Split my peanut butter Reece

BY DIANA THORNLEY

HALLWAY OF MESSAGES

ORIGINAL SONGS

BY DIANA THORNLEY

HALLWAY OF MESSAGES

DOWN ON MY KNEES TO YOU

Still on trial for a crime I didn't commit
I'm a prime suspect I must admit
I'm being abused for you feeling used
And accused of alleged desire
Your words slash through me like crackling
Thunder while I'm pronounced a convicted liar

CHORUS:
DOWN ON MY KNEES TO YOU
YOU GOT ME BEGGIN' YOU
DOWN ON MY KNEES TO YOU
I ONLY WANT YOU

You never give me a chance to explain
It's not the way that you think
My love for you is drowning in the rain
This thing we call love is on the brink

CHORUS:
DOWN ON MY KNEES TO YOU
YOU GOT ME BEGGIN' YOU
DOWN ON MY KNEES TO YOU
I ONLY WANT YOU

Your judge and jury better keep you warm at night
I won't be around cause you won't treat me right
No more
DOWN ON MY KNEES TO YOU

BY DIANA THORNLEY

HALLWAY OF MESSAGES

CONSUMMATION

Steamy letters
French perfume
Moans and cries
In the other room

Silky robes
French cologne
Sultry messages
On my answer phone

Urgent emotion
Extreme tension
Savior syndrome
Karmic redemption

CHORUS:
CONSUMMATION CONSUMMATION

Tender touch
Soft sensation
Sincere moves
Open invitation

Understanding
Exclusive relation
Heart and soul
Erotic elation

CHORUS:
CONSUMMATION CONSUMMATION

HALLWAY OF MESSAGES

Bitter words
Rapid flight
Spells of anger
White hot night

Pure white dove
Engagement ring
Everlasting love
The real thing

CHORUS:
CONSUMMATION CONSUMMATION

HALLWAY OF MESSAGES

BAT MEDICINE

Thought you'd be down at Bossa Nova's
I searched for you in the dark
Have you found the answer to life
in their secret dressing?
Ever looked for you in the park

Last time that I saw you
You looked so pale in the candlelight
Even through the last sensation
Somethin' was not quite right

CHORUS:
HABITS ARE CHANGIN'
YOU'RE REARRANGING
HABITS ARE CHANGIN'
CURED BY BAT MEDICINE

I wondered where you'd gone this time
to complete the journey of your soul
You know the way to your power
Only to abide this in my role.
In the bats shadow I stand alone
waiting to decide if your heart
has turned to stone

CHORUS:
HABITS ARE CHANGIN'
YOU'RE REARRANGING
HABITS ARE CHANGIN'
CURED BY BAT MEDICINE

HALLWAY OF MESSAGES

Like a bat that hangs upside down in a cave
You say your identity has got to change
So determined to transform yourself
You even put me upon a shelf

CHORUS:
HABITS ARE CHANGIN'
YOU'RE REARRANGING
HABITS ARE CHANGIN'
CURED BY BAT MEDICINE

HALLWAY OF MESSAGES

FRICTION

Are you liquid baby
Are you good to go
Can you give me what I want
Is what I wanna know

CHORUS:
WOO ME WITH EMOTION
COAX ME TO SUBMISSION
WATCHOO WAITIN' FOR
LET'S MAKE SOME FRICTION

Glitter isn't gold
Man build a house on a hill
Sill love you the same
But it don't give me a thrill
You blew a fuse
Now we're out like a light
Overpowered by emotion
On a cold Winter's night

(BRIDGE)

CHORUS:
WOO ME WITH EMOTION
COAX ME TO SUBMISSION
WATCHOO WAITIN' FOR
LET'S MAKE SOME FRICTION

HALLWAY OF MESSAGES

Your sorrow is your joy
In another reflection
If you don't like your life
Make another selection
Still waters run deep
How far can you go
You're asking me the question
But you don't wanna know

CHORUS:
WOO ME WITH EMOTION
COAX ME TO SUBMISSION
WATCHOO WAITIN' FOR
LET'S MAKE SOME FRICTION

Are you liquid baby
Are you good to go
Can you give me what I want
Is what I wanna know

CHORUS:
WOO ME WITH EMOTION
COAX ME TO SUBMISSION
WATCHOO WAITIN' FOR
LET'S MAKE SOME FRICTION

HALLWAY OF MESSAGES

KILLJOY

Sittin' outside the funeral parlor
Waitin' for a job interview
Dressed in black gloom intact
Had my cell so I thought I'd call you
Thought you'd be elated when I told you
The news 'bout the new high payin' job
You had your own separate views
Brand new position money for two
Guess it was all too morbid for you
I need someone alive to share
My nightmares too

CHORUS:
AH YOU'RE SUCH A KILLJOY
MAKIN' SUCH A SCENE
TURNED MY SWITCH FROM ON TO OFF
YOU AND YOUR ROUTINE

I strolled in sat right down
They asked me if I came from their side of town
I just gave them an inquiring line
The owner said I could never resign
I asked myself how many years
to the dead I could be true
let me go let me out forget this horrible zoo
I need someone alive to share
My nightmares too

HALLWAY OF MESSAGES

CHORUS:
AH YOU'RE SUCH A KILLJOY
MAKIN' SUCH A SCENE
TURNED MY SWITCH FROM ON TO OFF
YOU AND YOUR ROUTINE

I ripped the orchid from my hair
As I ran to escape the last cold stare
One thing I knew a better fate I was due
Next time I think a makin' money
I won't think of you
I need someone alive to share
My nightmares too

CHORUS:
AH YOU'RE SUCH A KILLJOY
MAKIN' SUCH A SCENE
TURNED MY SWITCH FROM ON TO OFF
YOU AND YOUR ROUTINE

HALLWAY OF MESSAGES

HEAL ME

When the Moon is
covered with darkness
All the stars will fall
Darkness descends
The howling winds
Will end

CHORUS:
HEAL ME
HEAL ME
HEAL ME

Your heart speaks
Eclipse of the soul
You envelop me
Equal control

CHORUS:
HEAL ME
HEAL ME
HEAL ME

HALLWAY OF MESSAGES

LAYIN' DOWN TRACKS

You won't stay away from the main line
Hittin' up your weekly fix
I gave you a caring compassionate sign
And better ways to get your kicks

CHORUS:
LAYIN' DOWN TRACKS

It's a hypodermic sensation
The rush you feel won't last
Once I was your savior
Now your brain cells are going fast

CHORUS:
LAYIN' DOWN TRACKS

Your body's resting at the terminal station
A symbol of the untamed youth
The destroying angel is your blood relation
Your system knows the truth

CHORUS:
LAYIN' DOWN TRACKS

There'll be a rage in heaven
As angels count your tracks
They'll count your number seven
Then slowly turn their backs

CHORUS:
LAYIN' DOWN TRACKS

HALLWAY OF MESSAGES

You don't even see
that those tracks baby
they don't lead to me

CHORUS:
LAYIN' DOWN TRACKS

HALLWAY OF MESSAGES

ABOUT THE AUTHOR

Diana Thornley also known as Rainy Knight grew up in a small Midwestern town. Needing space to grow she packed her bags and moved to Los Angeles in the mid-80s.

It was Los Angeles where she spread her wings and had a platform to grow as a creative artist. L.A. had the recording venues, clubs, and the people she needed to meet. Her music was played on six different states college radio and commercial radio.

Diana wrote poetry alongside her music in LA. Poetry and songwriting are natural cousins and she struck a balance. During her time in LA she had the good fortune of working with some big names in the industry including the late Ike Turner, the late Kim Fowley and Mike Pinera.

Her poetry has been published by the Famous Poets Society and soon to be released collective effort by Writing Rituals called Writing is our Superpower.

Diana has been featured in Music Connections, Easyriders, Autobuff, Wild Rag, Bam and Cosmo Chic magazines over the years. Her music can be found under Rainy Knight on her YouTube channel.

www.ingramcontent.com/pod-product-compliance
Lightning Source LLC
Chambersburg PA
CBHW072040060426
42449CB00010BA/2377